DARK WILD REALM

BOOKS BY MICHAEL COLLIER

POETRY

The Clasp and Other Poems (1986)

The Folded Heart (1989)

The Neighbor (1995)

The Ledge (2000)

Dark Wild Realm (2006)

TRANSLATION

Medea (2006)

PROSE

Make Us Wave Back: Essays on Poetry
and Influence (2007)

EDITED BY MICHAEL COLLIER

The Wesleyan Tradition: Four Decades
of American Poetry (1993)

The New Bread Loaf Anthology of
Contemporary American Poetry
(with Stanley Plumly) (1999)

The New American Poets:
A Bread Loaf Anthology (2000)

A William Maxwell Portrait: Memories
and Appreciations (with Charles Baxter
and Edward Hirsch) (2004)

DARK WILD REALM

Michael Collier

A MARINER BOOK

HOUGHTON MIFFLIN COMPANY

Boston · *New York*

First Mariner Books edition 2007
Copyright © 2006 by Michael Collier
ALL RIGHTS RESERVED

www.houghtonmifflinbooks.com

Library of Congress Cataloging-in-Publication Data
Collier, Michael, date.
Dark wild realm / Michael Collier.
p. cm.
ISBN-13: 978-0-618-58222-8
ISBN-10: 0-618-58222-3
1. Birds — Poetry. 2. Human-animal
relationships — Poetry. I. Title.
PS3553.O474645D37 2006
811'.54 — dc22 2005024759
ISBN-13: 978-0-618-91991-8 (pbk.)
ISBN-10: 0-618-91991-0 (pbk.)

Printed in the United States of America

Book design by Robert Overholtzer

WOZ 10 9 8 7 6 5 4 3 2 1

Katherine

CONTENTS

A PROLOGUE

The mind shapes bodies
that take on other shapes,
changes no one but gods should make.
And so I ask the gods
to let this song lead deftly,
back and forth through time,
until it finds the shape
of the world's beginning.

BIRDS APPEARING IN A DREAM

One had feathers like a blood-streaked koi,
another a tail of color-coded wires.
One was a blackbird stretching orchid wings,
another a flicker with a wounded head.

All flew like leaves fluttering to escape,
bright, circulating in burning air,
and all returned when the air cleared.
One was a kingfisher trapped in its bower,

deep in the ground, miles from water.
Everything is real and everything isn't.
Some had names and some didn't.
Named and nameless shapes of birds,

at night my hand can touch your feathers
and then I wipe the vernix from your wings,
you who have made bright things from shadows,
you who have crossed the distances to roost in me.

HOW SNOW ARRIVES

The pine trees stood without snow,
though snow was in the air,
a day or two away, forming in the place
where singing forms the air.

"Mother?" is what I heard my mother say,
said in such a way she knew *her* mother
didn't know her, as if they stood
beneath the trees and breathed the singing air.

How frail the weather when its face
is blank or, startled, turns to find
its startled self in a child's voice,
flake by flake of the arriving snow.

"Mother?" is what I say, as if
I didn't know her, standing blank
and startled where she stands beneath
the trees amid the singing air.

THE WATCH

Three days after our friend died,
having dropped to his knees
at the feet of his teammates,
we are sitting in a long,
narrow, windowless chapel,
staring at his casket
that runs parallel to the pews.
It's like a balance beam
or a bench you could sit on —
floral sprays around it,
a wooden lectern behind,
and a priest nobody knew,
a man I'd seen in the parking lot,
pulling on a beret and stamping out
a cigarette, all in one move,
as he emerged from his car,
holding a black book.
And now he is reassuring us
that our friend is in
a better place, that God,
too soon, has called him home,
a mystery faith endures.
Occasionally he looks down
to check his watch, the habit
of a man who always has
a next place to be, which must be why
he barely stays to finish the job.

                    Our friend
had the most beautiful voice
and his guitar was as cool
and smart, soulful
in its registers. When he played,
he gave his body to the music,
his eyes closed sometimes and his head bent,
sheltering what he made of himself,
his fingers knowing the next place
and the next—his voice, too—
taking each of us with him.

ABOUT THE MOTH

If you think the dead understand silence,
then why do they light their hems

and burn in dresses? Why do they fan their wings
against screens and windows as if they wanted in?

Why do they show their wiry contraptions
dusty with age and almost useless?

They only want to wake us with their light
unraveled from upper darkness.

They only want to hear us speak our reassurances.
Love will conquer, the heart endures.

And when they've left — flames, dust —
and frantic — we want them back,

not the friends and parents they once had been
but their new presences, sharp, unequivocal,

buoyant in their crossing back and forth,
inhabiting the condition they've become.

CONFESSIONAL

I was waiting for the frequency of my attention
to be tuned to an inner station — all mind but trivial matter,
wavelengths modulated like topiary swans on a topiary sea,
and not quite knowing where the tide would take me.

In the darkness where I kneeled, I heard whispering,
like dry leaves. It had a smell — beeswax, smoke;
a color — black; and a shape like a thumb.
That's when the door slid open and the light that years ago

spoke to me, spoke again, and through the veil,
an arm, like a hand-headed snake, worked through,
seven-fingered, each tipped with sin. What the snake couldn't see,
I saw, even as it felt what I felt or heard what I said.

Then along my arms boils and welts rose, on my back
scourge marks burned. I counted nails, thorns.
In my mind, inside my own death's head, I could hear: "Please,
forgive me. Do not punish me for what I cannot be."

SUMMER ANNIVERSARY

It was the night before the anniversary
of your death, and the dream I had
was not of you but of a neighbor
who the day before had undergone some tests.

He stood in his yard holding a rake
the size of a palm frond.
The grass was brown and the leaves
on all the trees hung as they do in summer,

patiently, not concerned they'll fall.
It was the night before the anniversary
of your death, and my neighbor with the rake
had not yet heard the results of his tests

and so he wanted to be ready for the leaves.
He wanted to apologize as well for being
in my dream. He said, "It's not like me
to die." "You're not dying," I told him,

"you're only in my dream." Then he disappeared.
But the rake he'd held stood by itself,
and the grass, now green, grew quickly
up the rake and sculpted a creature

whose wings stretched over me to catch
the falling leaves, for all at once
it was autumn and the sky let loose
its winter fox and then its hound,

though neither moved, and so the space between them
grew, slowly at first, until it was at the speed
of the world, unseen, spinning like time itself,
pushing apart lover and beloved.

BIRD CRASHING INTO WINDOW

In cartoons they do it and then get up,
a carousel of stars, asterisks, and question marks
trapped in a caption bubble above a dizzy,
flattened head that pops back into shape.

But this one collapsed in its skirt of red feathers
and now its head hangs like a closed hinge and its beak,
a yellow dart, is stuck in the gray porch floor
and seems transformed forever — a broken gadget,

a heavy shuttlecock — and yet it's not all dead.
The breast palpitates, the bent legs scrabble,
and its eye, the one that can't turn away,
fish-egg black, stares and blinks.

Behind me, sitting in a chair, his head resting
on a pillow, a friend recites *Lycidas* to prove
it's not the tumor or the treatment that's wasted
what his memory captured years ago in school.

Never mind he drops more than a line
or two. It's not a *lean and flashy song* he sings,
though that's what he'd prefer — his hair
wispy, his head misshapen.

Beyond the window, the wind shakes down
the dogwood petals, beetles drown in sap,
and bees paint themselves with pollen. "Get up! Fly away!"
my caption urges. "Get up, if you can!"

HOW DID IT GET INSIDE?

Not a message in a bottle
but the keel and wrongs,
the lap and brightwork,
beams and thwarts, and belowdecks,
in berths, hammocks hung.
Yardarms unfurled reefed sails.
Lines zinged through tackle.
Sizing stiffened the jib.
Hemp keelhauled pilferers
of the mess. But now it rides
at anchor in a dark room
where dust occludes the mind's eye.

Even so, you can hear
the deckhand's wooden leg,
like a butter churn, thump
to the memory of his sawed-off limb,
and the one-eyed crewmen gauge
the captain's rusted hook.
Somehow the corked-up wind
still swirls, the spinnaker bursts.
Speed moves the clouds
and the clouds disperse.
And the first mate's parrot,
wired to its perch, knows —
crow's nest to storm anchor —
once you've survived
the worst, the log records:
hope first, then skill.

TO THE MORTICIAN'S SON

No choice but to be your father's son
and yet never to be him, who moved like vapor,
who stood secure as a pillar,
and yet if not for you, prodigal,
stuffed in a dark suit,
if you had not tried to hand a program
to the deceased's ex
and usher her down the aisle like any mourner,
I would not find you consoling now,
not that I found you unsettling then,
or that your slovenly discomfort would be memorable,
especially the next day
when we interred my friend,
and you, positioned above the grave,
after a while made little steps
to move our small party down the hill
toward the black cars. Consoling
because my friend would have loved
how unfit you were for the family trade
and perhaps even enjoyed
how you peeved his former wife,
though not from malice,
and made of his death some melodrama,
human and absurd.

BOUGAINVILLEA

Of its productivity —
  whim of blossoming —
    hope that came

of its luck, of shade
  struck triumphantly:
    of this, so much worry.

Of its constant failure,
  travail trailing the tendering
    hand, and its rise by leaf,

through eave-height and sun-cower,
  the too much and too little,
    of its thirst;

from that was a life's consideration,
  the planted stave,
    the blessed frond replaced,

and of the cul-de-sac opening —
  the garden of one concern:
    gaudy mirror for the hummingbird,

bright reflection of stifled
  migration and the passage out.
    Of this was the perfume

and suffering,
  the blossom trained
    over all contingencies.

SNOW DAY

It's snowing and it won't ever stop!
In order for this to happen, the eastern tropics
of the Pacific have had to cool or warm.

Now the sun's not rising and the children,
still asleep, dream of weather as a rippling
curtain of northern lights across the arctic sky.

Or the children are awake and dressed
but have turned away from breakfast—
all the radios and all the televisions are on.

And even when the snow stops we will say,
It fell all day! Who cares if the sun rose
or the wind turned the trees to glass.

That's how snow is, falling, never stopping,
promising itself to itself, changing one day
into the same day, like happiness into happiness.

Now the sun is setting and the yard is blue.
And only someone who loves cold
and isolation could live like this,

waiting at the window for disturbance,
someone who wants the world buried,
who loves the short days, the deep long nights,

and then waking up to see nothing as it was
before the snow began to fall.

TWENTY-FIRST CENTURY

A lion is devouring a man.
That's how they first appear
when you come upon them
in the gallery, beneath the skylight,
among many other artifacts
removed from the past.

But the lion could as well
be kissing the man. The animal mouth
engaged with the throat, a leg
behind the neck, a paw gripping
biceps, supporting him
who in his pleasure tilts back

his head and spreads his legs,
but only so far as the lion allows,
for the lover's paw pins
the human foot, crushes
the toes and sandal of the man
who is ravished but not consumed.

THE MISSING MOUNTAIN

Cars could reach the mountain's saddle,
a notch between two peaks, and there
survey the grid of lighted streets,
a bursting net of beads and sequins,
a straining movement cruising for release.

"As far as the eye could see," though
few cared to look, was across the valley
to the other mountain, whose ridge
stood gaffed with broadcast towers, bright
harpoons quivering out our songs.

"Oh, wouldn't it be nice," the Beach Boys
harmonized. And it was. Sometimes I saw
the Milky Way invade the grid, Andromeda,
Draco, and great Betelgeuse bridging
the avenues and lanes, filling up acres

of vast parking lots. Sometimes I stared
powerfully into space where glowworms
of matter spun in pinwheels of gas.
What does it mean to be alive?
a voice asked. What does it mean

to have a voice speaking from inside?
Once I found a cockpit canopy from
a fighter jet in my neighbor's yard,
where it had fallen from the sky.
No one ever claimed it, such a large,

specific, useless thing, like the shoe
a giant leaves behind, like a mountain
from childhood — missing or pulverized —
it leaves a shape that once you see it
overwhelms the mind or makes a cloud

that is the shape of what the mountain was,
the sea floor covered with the sea.
"Oh, wouldn't it be nice," I used to sing,
and the mountains all around me answered,
but not the question I had asked.

SINGING, 5 A.M.

Yesterday when it began,
I think I laughed myself awake —
so perfect, and clear, so pre-recorded,
so much the birds of the neighborhood
doing what they're supposed to do.

And you waking next but not laughing,
not at all, not even aware yet
of how loud the morning was becoming.
But when I turned wanting to face you
and brushed your hip, we came alive
to the air — or the air enlivened us.

Well, it was dark. Neither of us could see,
though we were laughing,
which is what astonishment did to us,
even before we felt grateful
or dissatisfied, even before we knew
we'd been waiting — awake or asleep — for the birds,
so early and for what?

OUT OF WHOLE CLOTH

In the mirror above the sink
an open mouth sings
and a shower curtain breathes.

They're the elected delegates,
the weave and pattern,
of your own arabesque,

what fills the vessel
when the vessel's ready to be filled.
Water run over hands, and hands:

a cat's cradle,
a darn's cicatrix — a star
of the night's mending.

This is the shadow you put on,
the gown of torn sleep,
zippered and sleeveless, shawl

or towel, skin of your mother
or father that surrounds you
in the hours remaining.

THEIR WEIGHT

Swallows, phoebes, flycatchers,
chickadees, warblers,
and some terns and sparrows
are less than an ounce,

and are so little of water,
more hollow than bone,
though of substance
in boughs and leaves,

where they perch and fly,
for how little they want
of what matters, bright
and unmistakable — aspiring,

disappearing — not of who they are
but of what.

MINE OWN JOHN CLARE

He was the first person I knew who spoke to God
and to whom God replied. And he was the first person I knew
who had written the great works of whomever you might
 name —
mine own T. S. Eliot — though he affected no accent
and wore a shrunken Grateful Dead T-shirt.

It was not only madness that possessed him;
he had convictions and discernments, fine and fierce —
he rode a tricycle, small as it was,
back and forth from Pangaea to the End of the World
with a stop at the San Andreas Fault, where he lifted it,

wheels spinning, over the crack that runs to the center of the
 earth,
meaning he had circled all night in an empty parking lot
until his brother tracked him down and took him home.
He had moods and passions: months corresponding
with Germaine Greer and the articles he wrote for *Rolling Stone*

that appeared confoundedly under bylines not his own.
Once he spoke of walking three days from the northern high
 country
to the southern valleys, and toward the end, lost, hungry, he heard
a voice telling him to eat the grass. *Grass contains
the secret whisperings of love,* he said. But you had to crop

the tips of the blades and you had to be on your knees
with your head bowed and your eyes closed, and your lips made

the bitter taste sweet. Sometimes when he talked like this
he was also crying, because, he explained, *the grass contains wild
    onion*
and other truthful pungencies God requires me to eat.

And sometimes — *look at me!* — he'd put his face so close to
    mine
I no longer saw him but the parts that he contained: pores
and blemishes, the cheek's sharp contours, and his eyes,
dark, filmy patches, watery with years of homelessness ahead
but alive, fierce, and, as I pulled away, unforgiving.

ELEGY FOR A LONG-DEAD FRIEND

Last night when you appeared,
you brought the sacks of shoes
and folded clothes that stood
waiting in your garage
for someone else to remove
the day you died.

Because you were laid out
at the coroner's when I arrived
you couldn't know what I saw:
boots and sneakers, sandals
jammed in grocery bags, shirts
and pants no longer stylish.

Months before, what was it
you said? "Don't come around
here again." So why these visits?
Why the burden of this evidence?
And silent as you are,
does your presence mean forgiveness?

There was also, you should know,
a flat tire that gave your car
a slouched, defeated look.
I saw it before I saw the discards.
In Dante's hell the souls
spend their time repaying themselves

with their own sins. He witnessed
their anguish but was rarely moved,

and Virgil never. Next time
you visit, bring that tire,
wear it like a necklace,
and we'll set it on fire.

A WINTER FEEDING

After two days of snow,
sun, and then dozens
of robins landing in
the column-high trunk
of an oak shorn of limbs
but sheathed in vines —
and then a ravaging
of something unseen
that the leaves hide.

And that's how it felt
to have made the cold
surface of perfection
reflect the mind's
starving and brilliant
hunger, and then have
the world feed you
not only its remnants
of green but what

of winter light and coldness
clings as magnificence —
hollowed, truncated —
stilled by its own death,
undevoured, before
it calls down
the frenzied wings,
the starving beaks,
the ferrous breasts.

SPELUNKER

And you like a tongue
in the mouth of another

and you like a tongue

like a root given back
to the lips, to the petals

and stem of the flower.

And you a flower, a vine
squeezed through the attic,

white leaf and red foot,

splayed ear — a hand scraping
a rock. And there at the bottom,

the shore and the river,

the sky far above,
and you in the current,

in the lap and rush

of the dark, your head
bright with its lamp,

its light full of tremor.

THE MESSENGER

from Euripides' *Medea*

The moment your sons with their father
entered his bride's house, all of us,
who once served you and who mourned
your fate, were heartened. A shout went up —
you and Jason had called a truce.
This was like music to our ears. Suddenly
we wanted to kiss the children, touch their
lovely hair. Overwhelmed by happiness,
I followed them inside the princess's chambers.
We understood: she's the woman we must serve
instead of you.   At first she saw only Jason,
but when the children came into view,
she veiled her eyes and turned away.
Impatient with this display,
your husband scolded her, saying:
"Look at us. Don't revile your friends.
Your job is to love those your husband loves.
They've brought gifts. Accept them graciously
and for my sake ask your father to release
these children from their exile."

The gifts astonished her with their beauty.
She agreed to what her husband asked.
So eager was she to wear the treasures,
even before Jason and the boys had reached
the road, she put on the colorful dress,
set the gold crown on her head,
and in a bright mirror arranged her hair.
She laughed with pleasure at the beautiful

but lifeless image. Then, as if the gifts
had cast a spell, she stood up, traipsing
through her rooms, giddy with the feel of the gown,
twirling so she could see repeatedly
her shapely feet and pointed toes.

But quickly her face changed color. She staggered,
legs trembling, almost collapsing
before she reached a chair. One of the older, wiser
servants believed some wrathful god possessed her
and so cried out in prayer to Pan,
until she saw the mouth foaming,
eyes wild and rolling and skin leached of blood.
Then the prayers turned shrill with horror
and we servants raced to find Creon
and Jason to tell them the terrible news,
filling the house with the sound
of our panicked feet.

All of this happened in less time
than a sprinter takes to run the dash,
and quicker still was the way the princess
woke from her horrifying trance, eyes
wider than before, screaming
in anguish. For now a second torture
racked her. The gold crown exploded
in a fiery ring over her head, while
the delicate gown, brought by your sons,
ate into her sweet flesh. Consumed by flames,
she stood and ran, shaking her head
as if to throw the fire off, but the crown tangled
tighter in her hair and the blaze roared higher
as she fell to the floor and rolled

in the unquenchable flames.
Only her father could have known
who she was. The eyes had melted.
The face no more a face, while flaming blood
leaking from her head fueled the blaze.
But worse was how the flesh like tallow
or pitch sloughed off her bones.
All of this because the viperous poison
had locked her in its invisible jaws.

Schooled by what we'd witnessed, none of us
would touch the body, but her father
rushed to her side, not knowing what he'd find.
Nothing could prepare him for his daughter's
corpse. Misery broke from his voice.
He embraced and kissed her, lamenting,
"Unhappy child, murdered so shamefully,
why do the gods torture an old man like me?
Daughter, let me die with you."
But when his sobbing ceased
and old Creon wanted to rise, he found
he was woven to the fatal dress, stitched
to it like ivy to laurel, unable,
even as he wrestled furiously,
to free himself. The living father
who felt his flesh ripping from his bones
could not match the strength of his dead daughter,
and so he gave up and died, a victim
of her hideous fortune. Together now they lie
an old man and his daughter. Who wouldn't weep?

As for you, Medea, and your fate,
hear my silence. From it will come your punishment,

swift and sure. As for our brief lives, I've learned
once more we are mere shadows. No longer
do I fear to say the truth: fine words
and clever plans breed folly.
No man can count on his happiness.
Some have luck and fortune on their side
but never happiness.

A LINE FROM ROBERT DESNOS USED TO COMMEMORATE GEORGE "SONNY" TOOK-THE-SHIELD, FORT BELKNAP, MONTANA

I have dreamed of you so much,
you are the headless hawk
I found in a field, upturned
like a plow blade of feathers.
"Pick me up," you said, "so I might roost
as if I were the hawk."

I have dreamed of you so much,
a tree grew where I stood,
and grass rose up in flames
as if the hawk had sown a fire
from which its head appeared.
"Pick me up," it said.

I have dreamed of you so much
that now there is no dream,
no field or tree or fire,
only you roosting in the air.
"Pick me up," I say, "so I might roost
as if the world consumed my head."

BIGGAR, SCOTLAND, SEPTEMBER 1976

Our visit to MacDiarmid ended
with him drunk and asleep
at the end of an afternoon
in the cool, south-facing croft

and with his wife enraged
at our filling his glass
he held out begging
whenever she left the room,

yet how charming she'd been
about the Cornish and Welsh,
though not so charming
about the rest, while MacDiarmid

kept returning to the subject
of basalts — the ones on the Scottish
coast that matched ones in Canada.
But that was after he'd told us

about his trip to China with Greene
in the forties or fifties,
booze-fueled but still something
that had never lost its scent

as a dream. This man of science,
this communist, beautiful
in a starched white shirt,
who'd been propped up for us

in a chair, one hand cupping
an ear, the other clutching
a handkerchief, and his eyes
alive at the sight of your hair.

MEDEA'S OLDEST SON

I loved the sound of running water,
a fountain in winter, moss on the steps.
I'd gather pebbles from the courtyard
and drop them in the sacred well

to watch their colors change.
Time's portion was so small to me,
like the riffle of a current.
Water led me to her:

the way it moved with her anger,
also her love. My father kept a plan
inside his head. Its shape was like
the trellis where the birds nested.

In that world the children of demigods
were doomed, and if I survived,
who would be left to love?
No one knows anything until he dies.

The stones I dropped into the well
rest on the bottom, and the water
over them hasn't spoken, and so —
stone- and water-silent — and so, and so.

LOST HORIZON

They would come, blown off course, in their wheeling,
spiraling, then hovering, trash-like flocks,

and settle on the weekend seas of irrigated fields and parks,
like ducks on ponds too shallow for paddling —

or from a distance they might seem to float, though
in another sense held up by mirage and meniscus,

which meant you had to blink, refocus, to see what was
or wasn't there. Occasionally, in their midst

something bold, big-billed, and broad towered above them,
whose wings cast shadows large enough

to make its own weather, a foreigner among so many strangers.
And this was my first taste of the floods and plagues,

the rain that would not end over the unprepared lands.
And yet the birds, lifting one by one, retraced what they had
        been,

while filling up the emptiness they had made, returning
to wherever they had come, if such a place existed for so many.

AUBADE

Quietly the mornings used to start
as if the breath escaping from our mouths
was meant to fill the room
and that would be the day's requirement:

a volume equal to its space, arriving
as the sun arrived. Then we could hear
the sparrows fussing in the pyracantha,
the river of traffic from the freeway.

Then the wonder of the moment was that
the day made room for us at all.
But now we know the place, the numbered
hairs, and have seen the figures of ourselves

along the road, searching for the street
that leads into the avenues, then through
the intersections with their crossing guards.
Look how far into the day we've moved

and yet we're still in bed, awake, silent.
Escape or *stay* I used to tell myself,
waiting for you to shift and touch my leg
so I might turn to kiss your lips.

BOAT RENTAL

From the shore we could see the work it took to keep
the bow straight—constant adjudications
of wind and current. The boat, a kind of shuttle
threading elemental warp and woof. Each rower
faced the direction of his going, away from where he'd stood.
When the storm blew up they struggled to return.

Earlier, when it had been our turn and the water smooth
with intermittent scuds that slapped a beaver's tail
against the skiff, I thought, "Who doesn't love
the middle of his life?" My voice whispering
crucial adjustments, not anticipations
but greetings of air and water, mediums of resistance.

And then a man's voice, as if along a wire, traveled
from his mouth, in the middle of the lake, to my ear:
"Put your butt down, now!" Advice offered too late
to the tipping-over canoeist? Or from the shore,
more threatening, more resigned: "Why did we ever have
these children?"

A teenager soaked from a water fight screams
for the other teenager to stop his splashing.
He doesn't stop, and she wouldn't want him to, really.
Amid their laughter and commotion a flock of mallards
rises from stockades of bamboo on Duck Island,
circles eucalyptus and palms, and then returns.

What was once over the horizon is all around us.
The instruction in J-stroke not so much remembered

as imprinted — the saving gestures — and, of course,
the world divided between paddlers and rowers.
("There's room for a thermos and small ice chest.")
Few make a journey of diversion; most want a moment,

not a story. It felt good, then, to be afraid for others —
to see the storm approaching and the boats *racing*
for the dock. Finally, we all stood under the boathouse
and watched the vessels fill with rain. Those of us who were dry
were quiet, and those who were wet laughed,
uncertain if all the others had returned. Nevertheless,

we took pleasure in the cushions lifting off thwarts,
oars and paddles drifting away, the thermos bobbing,
while a plastic sack caught by its handles sang above us in a tree.

COMMON FLICKER

Old nail pounding your way
into bark or creosote,
intermittent tripod
of legs and beak,
derrick, larvae driller,

when I look up from
my mind I see what
you are: feather-hooded,
mustached, gripped
to the steady perch;

an idea of the lower
altitudes sparged
with color, a tuber
of claws and wings
and an eye unmarred.

Wing-handled hammer
packing the framer's blow,
face stropping the hardness,
drumming and drumming,
your song is your name.

This will cure me,
you declare. *This will*
heal the fractured jaw,
soothe the vibrating helve
so I can eat, so I can sing.

INVOCATION TO THE HEART

Speak to me now,
    alive, outside the body,
        massaged,

lifted from this package —
    rigged, hybridized,
        a chunk of sulfide

breeding worms —
    scorched, glittering,
        unburnable.

The severed veins are eyes,
    ears the pericardium.
        No longer

an abacus of click and slide,
    no longer the engine
        of this or that fist

but a machine of foreclosure,
    aurora of occluded sky,
        veil over the fetish.

Fill my mouth
    with imperfect speech.
        Remind me how you are

part pig, part parachute.
    Root in me, slow
        my fall.

Remember that each of us
     lay dead awhile
          waiting for the other.

A NIGHT AT THE WINDOW

The moth detaches from a leaf
and swims up through the dark
to flutter at the screen
through which the desk lamp shines.

You could almost say its wings
are oars, the legs like walking
rudders, except it doesn't float,
it skitters upward, out of sight,

and then returns, while the night
from which it's made withdraws,
and the light, a star so far above,
yet hot enough to burn, unwheels

its arms. Nothing stays, though
in a while the day comes on
and you can leave the window.
But who remains to watch

the navigating legs, the unfolded
sculling wings? What holds the place
until the night returns — the bang
and flutter — as if across the day

a face is formed, sun-drenched,
searching, wise with what it sees
and then unwise, caught
in its own light and then released.

THE LIFT

Birdsong in the morning air
and the whir of my neighbor's lift
as it raises him in his wheelchair
onto the bed of his truck.

Not someone to pity, he locks the wheels
in place and like a gymnast
on parallel bars manages himself
from his seat and then, in a move

too quick to see, disappears, though
because I've been there beside him
I know he's on all fours crawling
to the tailgate where he swings

over the edge and continues
in the dirt of the drive. Sometimes
when I'm weeding the garden
or admiring sunlight through leaves

the electric whir of the lift, followed
by its silence, breaks through and then
the hoof-slap of palms on the ground,
the scrape of shoes pulled along

by his strength, and I see him
as I did the first time, hoisting
a chainsaw, by block and tackle,
and then himself, into the blighted tree

towering between our yards
and which, limb by limb,
branch and trunk,
he cut down and stacked.

TO A CHAMELEON

After moving the clothes dryer to unclog the vent
I find your bracelet length of bone,
curve of vertebrae, spine
that is also tail, saurian claws
like clasps unclasped, and your skull
fallen away from its sharp neck.
It's harder now for you to understand,
harder for you to listen.
I once tried calling you back
with a pill cap of water, dead flies,
and something more absurd, a reptilian
whisper — all for my son's benefit,
who stood as still as you had stood,
leashed to his shoulder. And then
when unleashed you disappeared,
but left behind a writhing tail.
You were a lesson, at first, of love
that never repays itself and then
of absence and grief's forgetting,
but now what benefit is there
having found you, a fossil
unencumbered except by memory
and the sound of my son's breathing
and the chain and collar that still hangs
from your patient skeleton — the coppery
blue links and rusted white ash.

NIGHT STORY

There was an understanding of how the pages
of the book unfolded, like owl wings,
when my mother read to us, and how the words

of the familiar story, laid out in furrows,
skirted the farmyard—chickens, pigs, a tethered goat—
and lay like clouds over a billowing land,

or shadowed the white house with black lightning rods
while parked near the shed stood a truck as old as a grandfather.
Night, dark earth, brought darker clouds.

Lightning flashed. A red tractor, all but its nose
in the barn. Calm and clear and plain,
my mother urged the boy out into the thunder

and rain to drive the animals back to their coops
and stalls. Hair stood on end. My sister squirmed.
The great chestnut tree split, caught fire. Half

fell in the pond where the flames soon died
and half fell on the barn. All of this so long ago
a boy could reach the blackened tractor

without anyone saying, "It's only a story,
life doesn't happen this way."
But how else did hair rise on my arms the first

and last time the story was read? And what woke
my sister from her dream where she stood
in a forest, burning, among an alphabet of flames?

TURKEY VULTURES

The red drill of their faces, pink-tipped,
grubbed in gore, cyclopean in their hunger
for the dead but not the dying, lugubrious
on their perches from towers, in trees, where they
convene like ushers on church steps.

Heads sculpted to fit cane handles, claws
to dibble seed, to sort out the warp of sinew
from the woof, unwind the gray bobbins of brain.
Assiduous as cats as they clean, wing scouring
wing, until the head polished like a gem

gleams, and the ears no more than lacy holes
are sieves for passing air or molecules of gas.
These birds, who wear the face of what will last,
congregating but not crowding, incurious
and almost patient with their dead.

IN MAY

In May the paths into the dunes
are roped off from foot traffic
because the birds amass to breed.

You can watch them through binoculars
from the edge of a parking lot,
white invisible deltas that drop

and glint, cataractous floaters
against the sun, rising from the sea
or fluttering midday from nests

spiked inside the broken clumps
of compass grass. Or on a plaque
read about a lighthouse stretched

like bones beneath the waves.
When Heraclitus observed,
"You can't step into the same river twice,"

did he mean you couldn't trust
experience or thought to illustrate
how "nature loves to hide" beneath

its own swift surface? Did he mean
there's pleasure in deception,
not despair, delight when we recognize

a tern's or plover's flash and glitter,
silhouettes that navigate thermal rivers,
declare themselves like scraps of paper,

then disappear?

SHELLEY'S GUITAR

How much more beautiful it is
because it's Shelley's guitar —
a coffin of trapped song
in a body like a grave.

Because it's Shelley's guitar
it's been put on display,
a case within a case,
a wooden hand inside a velvet glove,

and nearby, the torn copy of *Adonais*
that held his heart for thirty years.
Next to it, other incomparable relics:
his baby rattle, a watch, the plate

off which he ate the beautiful
raisins of his diet. Everything
encased, preserved, though
the heart now is only a stain, a watermark

on pages his widow used to save it.
Never mind the guitar was given to his friend
Jane, as if it were the heart
unauctioned, a neck

with tuning pegs, gut strings, arabesque
filigree. And never mind the guitar
was meant to be a pedal harp
he couldn't afford. "Take this slave

of music," the poem says, "for the sake
of him who is the slave of thee."
Whose heart is it but Shelley's?
Whose grave, whose book, whose glove and raisins?

All those things that have been given
either by "action or by suffering,"
left behind, collected, to prove
the dead have substance.

BARDO

Dangerously frail is what his hand was like
when he showed up at our house,
three or four days after his death,
and stood at the foot of our bed.

Though we had expected him to appear
in some form, it was odd, the clarity
and precise decrepitude of his condition,
and how his hand, frail as it was,

lifted me from behind my head, up from the pillow,
so that no longer could I claim it was a dream,
nor deny that what your father wanted,
even with you sleeping next to me,

was to kiss me on the lips.
There was no refusing his anointing me
with what I was meant to bear of him
from where he was, present in the world,

a document loose from the archives
of form — not spectral, not corporeal —
in transit, though not between lives or bodies:
those lips on mine, then mine on yours.

THE NEXT NIGHT

I found my way back
by grief scent and smoke
to the daughter's voice
from the father's mouth.

This time you asked
that I step outside my body,
though not far enough to fall
into the abyss of night

or near the flames
that ringed the bed.
I couldn't say "Go away,"
because the dead can hear,

and they, as you remind, float
above us, not everywhere,
but here and there, following
their own preoccupations.

Besides, I loved your skirt
of burning tongues,
the sleeveless blouse that fit you
as it fit the armless mannequins.

I loved all the shibboleths
for torture, all the archaic
pleading that made you
smother what I tried to say

by saying, "Come with me,
inhabit the inch of air
between our forms and their
vaporous happenstance."

But no one talks like that,
not even the dead when they speak
through you, though
it's what I heard floating in the spaces.

It's what fed the flames
of your command
that all of me resisted
even as I followed.

NOTES

"A Prologue." After Ovid's *Metamorphoses,* lines 1-24.

"The Watch." Dedicated to the memory of Dennis Casey.

"Bird Crashing into Window." A phrase from line 123 of *Lycidas* is incorporated into line 18. Dedicated to the memory of Agha Shahid Ali.

"The Messenger." Lines 1136–1230 of Euripides' *Medea.*

"A Line from Robert Desnos Used to Commemorate George 'Sonny' Took-the-Shield, Fort Belknap, Montana." George Took-the-Shield was fifty-three when he died of cancer. He was an Assiniboin who was instrumental in repatriating his ancestors' remains held by the Smithsonian Institution. He was an artist, writer, and poet.

"Biggar, Scotland, September 1976." Hugh MacDiarmid (1892–1978) was the pen name of Christopher Murray Grieve, Scotland's greatest poet of the twentieth century. His masterpiece is the 2,685-line *A Drunk Man Looks at the Thistle* (1926).

"Invocation to the Heart." Pig ventricular valves and nylon are materials used to repair the human heart.

"Shelley's Guitar." *Shelley's Guitar: A Bicentenary Exhibition of Manuscripts, First Editions and Relics of Percy Bysshe Shelley* was sponsored by the Bodleian Library, 1992. The lines quoted in the poem are from "With a guitar. To Jane," which Shelley wrote for Jane Williams.

"Bardo." Dedicated to the memory of Ben Branch.

ACKNOWLEDGMENTS

GRATEFUL ACKNOWLEDGMENT to the editors of the publications where the following poems first appeared: *Agni Review*, "Spelunker," "Invocation to the Heart." *Alaska Quarterly Review*, "Boat Rental." *Atlantic Monthly*, "Bardo." *Bellevue Review*, "How Snow Arrives." *Blue Mesa Review*, "A Night at the Window." *Georgia Review*, "To a Chameleon," "Summer Anniversary," "Twenty-first Century." *Grove Rerview*, "Aubade," "How Did I Get Inside?," "Medea's Oldest Son," "Night Story," "The Watch." *Gulf Coast*, "Elegy for a Long-Dead Friend." *Kenyon Review*, "Snow Day," "The Missing Mountain," "Confessional," "Bird Crashing into Window," "*Lost Horizon.*" *The Nation*, "In May." *Ploughshares*, "The Next Night," "Their Weight," "Mine Own John Clare," "Birds Appearing in a Dream," "A Line from Robert Desnos Used to Commemorate George 'Sonny' Took-the-Shield, Fort Belknap, Montana." *Rivendell*, "A Winter Feeding." *Slate*, "Shelley's Guitar," "The Lift." *Sonora Review*, "Bougainvillea," "Out of Whole Cloth Made." *TriQuarterly*, "Common Flicker," "Turkey Vultures." "Common Flicker" also appeared in *The Best American Poetry 2007*, edited by Heather McHugh.

I wish to thank the University of Maryland for a creative and performing arts summer grant, which contributed to the completion of this book, and Middlebury College for its ongoing support.

My gratitude, thanks, and affection go to Liz Arnold, Daniel Hall, Edward Hirsch, Jim Longenbach, Tom Mallon, John Murphy, Howard Norman, Steve Orlen, Stanley Plumly, Buzz Poverman, Michael Ryan, Alan Shapiro, Tom Sleigh, Elizabeth Spires, Ellen Bryant Voigt, Josh Weiner, and Dean Young.

In memory: Agha Shahid Ali, Ben Branch, Dennis Casey, Amanda Davis, Roland Flint, William and Emily Maxwell, Mike Powell, Carl Richardson, and George Took-the-Shield.

And with love to David and Robert.

ABOUT THE AUTHOR

MICHAEL COLLIER is the director of the Bread Loaf
Writers' Conference and teaches English at the
University of Maryland, College Park. He has published
four previous collections of poetry, most recently
The Ledge, a finalist for both the Los Angeles Times
Book Prize and the National Book Critics Circle Award.
Collier is the recipient of a Guggenheim fellowship,
NEA fellowships, and the Discovery/The Nation Award,
among other honors, and is a former poet laureate
of Maryland. He lives in Maryland.